CONGRATULATIONS!

YOU MAY HAVE ADHD.

That's okay. Lots of people do.

You're going to be fine.

BUT DO NOT TURN THE PAGE!
INSTEAD, FLIP TO PAGE 23.

NOT THIS PAGE!

Don't like to follow directions, do you? We understand.
GO TO PAGE 23 ANYWAY.

Please...

Cosworth Publishing
21545 Yucatan Avenue
Woodland Hills CA 91364
www.cosworthpublishing.com

For information regarding permission,
please send an email to office@cosworthpublishing.com.

The Attention Deficit Disorder Hyperactive Cookbook

Puzzle Edition

Jimmy Huston

WHAT IS ADD? (OR IS IT ADHD?)

ADD is short for Attention Deficit Disorder, a condition that causes some people to be inattentive, easily distracted, or subject to memory problems.

Because some people with ADD are also hyperactive (fidgety) or impulsive, ADD is now called ADHD, which stands for Attention Deficit Hyperactivity Disorder — whether you are hyperactive or not.

It can be confusing, like if you said peanut butter sandwiches and peanut butter and jelly sandwiches were now both to be called peanut butter and jelly sandwiches, but divided into sandwiches with jelly and without jelly. Makes perfect sense.

This means you can have ADHD without being hyperactive. That's the daydreamer, who is inattentive. Or, you can be the fidgeter, who can't stay still, but also is inattentive.

In other words...

FROM PAGE 55

GO TO PAGE 10

ADHD ISN'T NEW. IT'S BEEN AROUND FOR A LONG, LONG TIME.

Over centuries, many people have been affected by it, and while it can be difficult, many of them have accomplished great things.

Many successful people happily admit to their ADHD tendencies, and often give them credit for contributing to their success. You're going to see many examples. You may not yet know who some of them are, but you will.

You might know some of these famous people who freely talk about their ADHD: Adam Levine, Justin Timberlake, Paris Hilton, Channing Tatum, Zooey Deschanel, will.i.am, Emma Watson, Woody Harrelson, Justin Beiber, and Ryan Gosling.

Don't worry. You don't have to be an actor or entertainer. You'll see others on other pages.

FROM PAGES 20, 26, & 40

ADHD ISN'T GOING TO STOP YOU.

Although there's no way to test for ADHD in someone a hundred or more years ago, people talk about historical figures and study them and write about them. Often they are known to have habits and behaviors that are good clues.

For instance, it is believed that Christopher Columbus had ADHD. And Socrates. Also Nostradamus. Winston Churchill, too. They did okay. You will, too.

GO TO PAGE 30

AM I A FREAK?

No.

You are not a freak. You are simply a person with a problem. Everyone has problems. Your problem has a name, and you can learn to deal with it. You're going to be fine.

ADHD is common. Look around you. The odds are there is probably someone in your class dealing with ADHD. It may even be the teacher. Don't be afraid to talk to that person about how to deal with ADHD.

About 5% of the world's population have some form of ADHD. That's one in twenty people — one in twenty KIDS.

There are about eight billion people in the world. Five percent is 400,000,000 people. You are not alone.

Every one of those eight billion brains is different. Some are typical. Some are unusual.

If you are one in four hundred million people with ADHD, you are not a freak.

FROM PAGE 6

Getting Bored? Take a break!

Go outside and play for a while.

Then come back and turn to PAGE 48

5

From Page 11

Will Medicine Help?

Medicine can help, but there is no single answer to ADHD. Drugs that help some people do not help others.

Oddly enough, medicines that are stimulants can sometimes calm kids with ADHD. Some non-stimulant medicines can also help. Antidepressants are also used in some cases.

Your doctor may try several medicines at different dosages to find what helps you.

It's important to tell your doctor how the medicine makes you feel. That helps the doctor know how to adjust your dosage, or perhaps even to change medications altogether.

Also, some kids with ADHD stop taking their medications after a few months. Because ADHD is chronic, it is necessary for medication to be taken consistently to be effective, so don't cheat.

There is evidence that vitamins and minerals can have a positive affect on kids with ADHD. It is thought that low levels of some neurotransmitters in the brain are related to the development of ADHD, and that these micronutrients can help.

Some experts believe that a proper diet of fruits and vegetables can provide the same benefit.

Also, get plenty of sleep.

RECIPE

1 Pill
1 Glass of Water

Swallow Pill.
Sip Water.
Repeat As Directed.

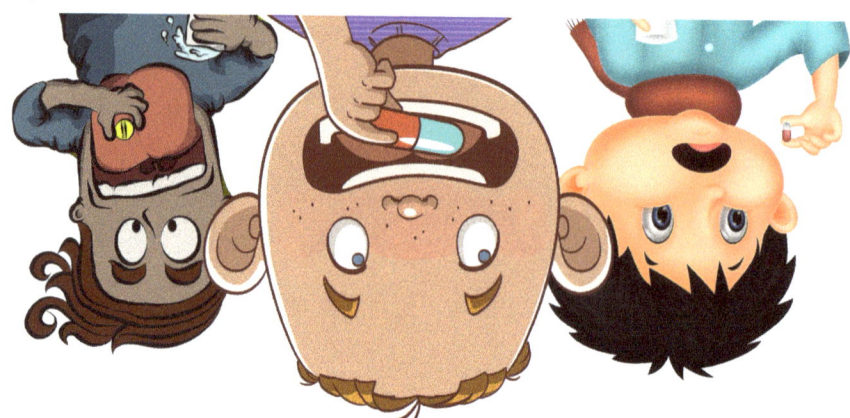

Go to Page 4

How Did I Get It?

You were born with it. ADHD is not contagious. No one can "catch" it from you, you can't give it to anyone, and it is not caused by watching TV, playing video games, or too much sugar.

ADHD is believed to be genetic in nature, which means you probably inherited it, although it's possible that it is affected by environmental factors, nutrition, or injuries.

Some doctors believe that one factor is reduced dopamine, a chemical in the brain that can help move signals between nerves.

TIME IS DIFFERENT WITH ADHD.

There are three kinds of time. There's AM time, PM time, and ADHD time.

Time is a variable speed phenomenon for kids in the ADHD Club. It just flows differently for you.

There is no real "sense" of time. It's there. It isn't there. Whatever. Maybe it's important. Sometimes. But maybe not.

Do you feel like two minutes is basically the same as two months? That can be a problem, whether you're boiling a three-minute egg or trying to catch the school bus early in the morning. Do you always misjudge the amount of time a task will take (or a tomato)?

Life is hard when you're always fighting the clock.

Teach yourself to pay attention to time.

FROM PAGE 57

GO TO PAGE 14

SPINNERS?

Not so fast!

Fidget spinners have been heralded as a way to channel excess energy and reduce ADHD stress in some kids. Many teachers disagree. They find them distracting to everyone, including the kids spinning them.

YEAH, IT'S A BRAIN THING.

ADHD is neurodevelopmental. That means as you grow, your brain develops in a way that can cause difficulty with learning, memory, self-control, behavior, emotions, and language.

That makes some things harder for you than for other people, especially things that require concentration — like that pesky old schoolwork.

Your brain sometimes has trouble controlling thinking, paying attention, and planning things, but it's the only brain you get so you need to find a way to work with it.

FROM PAGE 1

IT STARTS EARLY.

Babies are a lot of work. ADHD babies are even more work. That's when some parents begin to suspect they have a child with ADHD, usually by comparing behaviors to other children the same age.

Early identification and treatment is critical. Otherwise, problems can develop such as trouble at school, stress at home, people problems, depression, substance misuse, and possible injuries. Symptoms can occur as early as age 2 and can continue into adulthood, changing with age.

Find the ADHD tools early and make your life easier.

GO TO PAGE 6

If there's no cure, what can I do?

It may sound silly, but there are ordinary activities that could help. Doing things can relax your brain or engage it creatively. It also drains excess energy so you can think. Try some of these things.

Do you enjoy music? Listen to some.

Play a game that relaxes you.

Do you have a pet? Play with it.

If you play an instrument or sing, perform your favorite song. Get loud!

Try dancing, either alone or with partners. Get wild!

Draw something or paint a picture.

Clean up your room. (Try it.)

Go for a walk.

Run during your "walk."

If you like to cook or bake, make something — like cookies — then eat them. Or give them to friends.

Ride your bike or skateboard.

Make up a silly play or skit. Perform it for your family or friends. Have some fun.

When any of these things work, remember them and use them as tools when you're having problems.

From Page 39

Go to Page 36

13

You are not the problem...

But you already knew that. You're fine.

Your parents are the problem. And your teachers. And even your friends.

Your parents expect you to ignore all your impulses to do what you want to do, and instead they want you to do what they want you to do. That doesn't seem fair.

Your teachers want you to act like everybody else acts. But you aren't like everybody else. You're you!

Some of your friends may think you're weird. So what? You're you, and if they want to be your friend, they should take you as you are.

Sounds good, huh?

But it doesn't work like that.

You have to live in the same world as everyone else, like it or not.

You need your parents and your teachers and your friends. Things will get better if you work with them. Try to see things from their point of view. Find some middle ground.

Most of all, listen to what people are saying. You may learn some ways to please them that will make your life easier.

They're all probably telling you what you're doing "wrong" — in their opinion. Try to work toward the things they suggest. Try some small steps, just to keep the peace.

Pay attention to what's going on. If you ask questions, it may help you understand. It may help you stay interested.

FROM PAGE 9

Maybe strike a deal with your parents. You'll try to do what they want you to do, if they promise to give you time for your own thoughts — your own adventures and explorations.

Maybe you don't put off your homework too long. See if it makes it easier to start earlier.

...You Are the Solution

If it's hard for you to sit still, do something you can do sitting down.

Write a poem. Or a song. Or a book. Draw a picture.

If you need to get up, and you're where that is appropriate, get up and do something worth doing. Use up some of that hyperactive energy.

Make a video. Dig a hole. Chase a bird. Wash the family car. Learn to knit. Smell some flowers.

Oh, and cook something. This is a cookbook, after all.

Go to Page 16

DO COMPUTER GAMES CAUSE OR WORSEN ADHD?

No.

Your parents probably complain that you can play computer games for hours, but you can't focus on schoolwork or chores.

Well, these games keep your attention because they keep changing constantly and the tasks are quickly done. Something is always happening, requiring short bursts of attention and providing constant stimulation and instant rewards. It's fun!

The problem with computer games is they rob your time from your schoolwork — so find a happy medium and do both.

Maybe your school should be using computer games to teach math and history and science.

There is an FDA-authorized video game that is a treatment for ADHD and is even covered by some medical insurance plans. Wow!

FROM PAGE 15

IS THIS REALLY A COOKBOOK?

Not exactly. Maybe you should just make a sandwich.

Meanwhile, it's time to make a choice.

GIRLS ONLY,
GO TO PAGE 20

BOYS ONLY,
GO TO PAGE 26

PARENTS ONLY,
GO TO PAGE 40

Art and ADHD Go Together

Throughout history there have been artists who had many characteristics of ADHD, yet were prolific and accomplished.

Pablo Picasso's outrageously provocative paintings were the hallmarks of the cubist art style.

Salvador Dali was a surrealist artist who worked in a wide range of different media.

Vincent Van Gogh was a misunderstood genius whose paintings are among the most expressive art ever created.

Leonardo da Vinci was a brilliant painter and sculptor, but is equally well known for exploring architecture, engineering, science, and other interests. Francois Auguste Rodin broke new ground in sculpture and was considered the master of his time. Ansel Adams, a pioneer in photography, specialized in magnificent landscapes that revealed the beauty of America.

FROM PAGE 43

18

Writers are pretty smart. They are thinkers, first of all. They build entire worlds and create characters that fascinate millions of readers. Some of the greatest writers of all time are believed to have had ADHD. That didn't stop them.

How many of these do you know? Hans Christian Anderson, Jules Vern, Agatha Christie, F. Scott Fitzgerald, Ralph Waldo Emerson, Virginia Woolf, Walt Whitman, Lord Alfred Tennyson, George Bernard Shaw, Tennessee Williams, and Robert Frost.

Go to Page 50

FROM PAGE 17

FOR GIRLS ONLY.

Girls are less likely than boys to have ADHD. They are even less likely still to be diagnosed with ADHD.

Girls are usually not disruptive.

They are more likely to be inattentive rather than hyperactive, but hyperactivity is a possibility nevertheless.

Often they are just thought to simply be shy or introverted, so they don't get the same attention to their ADHD, when therapies or medication could be helpful.

Do you daydream frequently?

Do people say you're overly emotional?

Are you a hyper-talker?

Sometimes ADHD can result in depression or anxiety. Don't be afraid to talk to someone. You can get help.

GO TO PAGE 2

WELCOME. GLAD YOU COULD MAKE IT.

This book is for you.

It is not for your parents, your teachers, your coaches, your doctor, your chef, your siblings, or your friends.

If any of them want to read it, charge them a dollar.

When they try to ignore that, tell them it's for your retirement fund.

They will probably smile, and — if you stick to it — they just might pay you.

It's worth a try....

23

SO NOW GO TO PAGE 54

WHAT ABOUT MY OTHER PROBLEMS?

It's not unusual for kids with ADHD to have other issues that make it hard to diagnose and treat everything.

Think of ADHD as a soup. The other issues are like spices that can change the soup.

Together, any number of these things can combine with ADHD to make a difficult soup.

FROM PAGE 59

GO TO PAGE 28

FOR BOYS ONLY.

Easily distracted? Difficulty paying attention? Are you still reading this?

There are about three times more boys with ADHD than girls.

There's a wide range of symptoms for boys. Are you inattentive? Or, do you hyperfocus on things that interest you? You can do both of those, even though they are completely opposite things.

Do you focus on little things and miss the big picture? Do you have trouble understanding how much time a task will take? Do you over-react to things — or under-react?

FROM PAGE 17

Boys are more likely to have hyperactive aspects of ADHD, but you already knew that.

Maybe you're fidgety.

Or you're impulsive.

You can't stop moving.

You have issues with self-control. Maybe your teachers are getting tired of your acting up in class.

There are solutions that can help. Medicine. Therapy. Exercises.

Boys are also much more likely to be prescribed medicine (partly because they're more likely to need it). It can really help.

Therapy can help you understand what's going on, how it affects others, and how it affects you.

Exercises can help you deal with problem issues, such as time management, anger issues, and memory problems.

Don't be afraid to ask for help.

GO TO PAGE 2

BAD THINGS CAN SOMETIMES BE GOOD — IN MODERATION.

A touch of being obsessive-compulsive might just give you the drive and concentration to follow a project through to the ending.

Hyperactivity can provide energy to get things done.

A little procrastination can allow time for planning and developing thoughts.

But obsessive compulsion might endlessly chop up ingredients and overfill the pot.

Hyperactivity might add too many ingredients or overstir the soup and send it splashing onto the stove or floor.

Too much procrastination and the soup is never finished.

Each of these ingredients must be limited to "just the right amount."

Successful people with ADHD have harnessed the traits that can be useful and put them to work. You can, too.

FROM PAGE 25

THE ADHD COOKBOOK
ADHD TEST

Do you think you have it?

YES ☐   NO ☐

Do your parents think you have it?

YES ☐   NO ☐

Do your teachers think you have it?

YES ☐   NO ☐

If you're reading this, you probably have it.

YES ☐   NO ☐

If someone is making you read this, you definitely have it.

YES ✅   NO ☐

That's okay.

Just keep reading.

GO TO PAGE 38

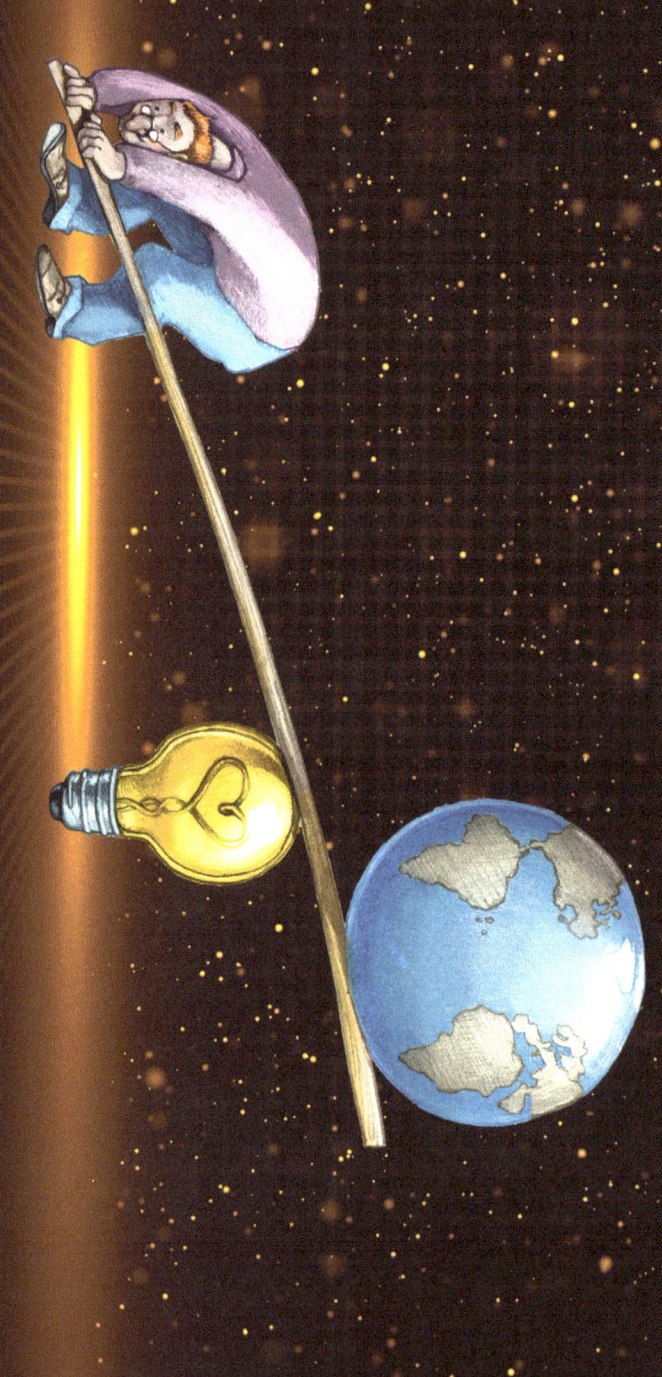

The world as we know it today has been explained to us down through history by the great thinkers of science. Using the tools of their day, they have made discoveries and created theories that changed our understanding of the universe.

Some of these great thinkers have shown telltale signs of ADHD in their lives, perhaps things that aided their imagination.

Galileo Galilei began describing the universe with early telescopes. Isaac Newton developed our understanding of gravity. Wernher von Braun guided the development of our early spaceships. Albert Einstein pioneered the theory of relativity and explored the theory of quantum mechanics. Stephen Hawking studied black holes from a wheelchair and explained theories of the universe to the public.

From Page 3

Everyone says they want kids to be creative. By definition creativity is outside of normal, average, everyday thoughts. That's when creative thoughts can come up.

Einstein, Newton, and Archimedes all three were believed to have ADHD. Neither of them were working in an academic setting when they had the significant breakthroughs that made them seem brilliant.

Legend says Archimedes was getting into his bath when the water overflowed, inspiring Archimedes' Principle, a fundamental law of physics regarding buoyancy.

As the story goes, Newton was under the proverbial apple tree when a falling apple hit him in the head, causing him to begin to understand the concept of gravity.

They say that Einstein was riding on a bus when he had the breakthrough brainstorm that led to e-mc², whatever that really means.

GO TO PAGE 32

JUST FOR FUN, TRY BECOMING PRESIDENT OF THE UNITED STATES.

Three of the four presidents on Mount Rushmore are believed to have had ADHD: Abraham Lincoln, Thomas Jefferson, and Theodore Roosevelt. (George Washington didn't, but he may have had dyslexia.)

Other presidents believed to have had ADHD were Dwight D. Eisenhower, John F. Kennedy, and Woodrow Wilson.

So ADHD is not an excuse. You can work through it and find your own success. If you make it to becoming President of the United States, we'll add you to the list — maybe even to Mount Rushmore — but that's not the goal.

Happiness is the goal. Everyone has problems. If ADHD is one of yours there is every reason to think you'll find success in your life. And happiness.

FROM PAGE 31

TAKE ANOTHER BREAK

Here's a space to draw or paint something. (It's your book, so you're allowed to draw in it.) Or write something if you prefer. Or tear out the page and make a paper airplane.

GO TO PAGE 34

If you made a paper airplane out of the previous page, then this page is gone. You might want to draw or color on it first. Or not.

Your choice.

FROM PAGE 33

MANY MUSIC GIANTS ARE ADHD!

Match the picture to the names.
George Frideric Handel
Stevie Wonder
Ludwig Von Beethoven
Justin Bieber
John Lennon
Kurt Cobain
Wolfgang Amadeus Mozart
Elvis Presley

Then go get your guitar, or play
your piano, or write a song.
Sing it loud!

Go to Page 42

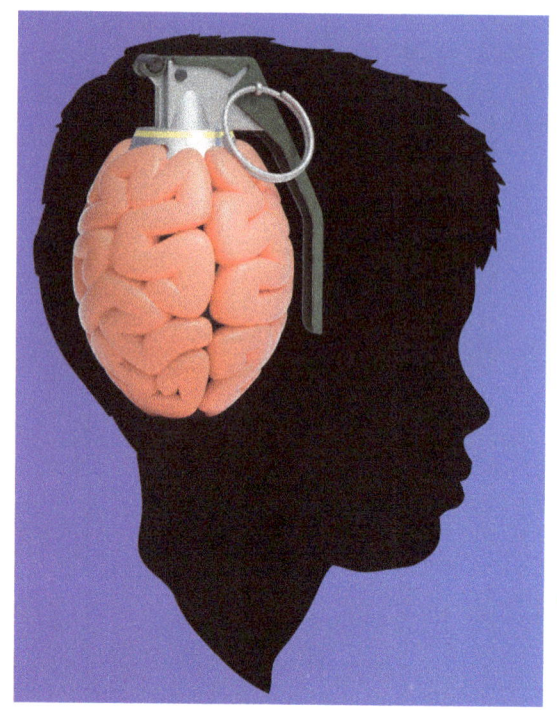

IMPULSIVENESS CAN BE A HANDFUL OF TROUBLE.

A failure to think things through before you jump in can create a lot of problems for you and others, all the way up to injury or worse.

Even a hand grenade has a fuse. Dynamite has a fuse, and for good reason.

Before impulsively doing something try imagining a fuse that will give you time to think. Consider the consequences of every action. Will you or someone else get hurt? Or embarrassed?

Will something unpleasant happen?

Slow down. Think it through!

2 cups salt
1 cup pepper
1 pint apple cider vinegar or lemon juice
1/2 cup basil, thyme, oregano or whatever.
17 avocados

Put the broth in a big ol' pot. Turn it all the way up.
Sauté chopped celery, onion, & carrots in olive oil.
Or don't bother. Throw it in.
Add garlic to the saute. Too late. Throw it in, too.
Throw away any broccoli, cauliflower, or squash.
Add everything else. Fast as you can.
Stir it, unless you're busy with something else.
Simmer for 3 days.
Or order a pizza!

FROM PAGE 13

ADHD can cause social anxiety because you are not like other kids. ADHD can cause social issues, and at the same time is affected by social issues — because your impulsiveness may mean you can't moderate social behaviors.

Kids with ADHD often hit a new project or activity at full speed, and they can do the same thing to new friends, hyperattaching to new people. Do you always think you've found your new best friend? Do you quickly hurry into telling secrets or over-sharing your life. Are you overly sensitive to perceived social slights?

Sometimes you just move too fast — even talking too fast, anticipating where the conversation is going when it may not be going there at all. Your super-fast thoughts can move too quickly and your statements may seem random and even shocking to your friends who just don't understand the jumps that your brain speed causes.

GO TO PAGE 56

Hyperactive Vegetable Soup Recipe

Think big! Make a lot and make it fast!

33 quarts of chicken broth or vegetable broth
31 carrots (chopped)
27 cups of pinto beans
35 cups of corn (fresh, frozen, or canned)
40 large tomatoes (chopped)
27 stalks of celery (chopped)
12 bell peppers (chopped)
26 potatoes (diced)
21 onions (diced)
40 cloves garlic (chopped)
20 tbsp olive oil

FROM PAGE 29

38

Time Management
and Disorganization Troubles?

Kids with ADHD often have issues with time management and organization.

Time is discussed both seriously and whimsically by philosophers, novelists, astronomers, and physicists.

Have you already read that sentence before? No? Oh, here it is...

Time is discussed both seriously and whimsically by philosophers, novelists, astronomers, and physicists.

See? It happened again. Time travel? Sort of.

If it's good enough for philosophers, astronomers, novelists, and physicists to play with time, it's good enough for kids with ADHD.

Daydreaming isn't all bad.

Albert Einstein was known for his extremely messy desk. Should he have spent his time cleaning up? What about Thomas Edison? Ditto. Or Steve Jobs? Double ditto.

So you're disorganized and forgetful. So what?

Go to Page 12

To Parents.

Granted, it's not easy being a parent — especially the parent of a kid with ADHD.

But — this is not about you! This is a struggle for your kid. One way to help is to try to imagine what it's like from his or her point of view.

Imagine — the grownups in your world always want you to do things that you don't want to do. Some are difficult, some are unpleasant, and some are really, really boring. At the same time there are lots of other things flashing through your mind.

Your kid needs more encouragement than criticism. Reward positive behaviors immediately. Provide consequences when appropriate. Then, more encouragement.

Stay in touch with your kid's teachers. Suggest things that can help, such as developing routines and schedules, allowing time for physical movement, offering encouragement, helping with organizational skills, and understanding self-esteem issues.

There are not really any magic medications for parents of ADHD kids, but there is therapy. Don't count that out. Family therapy can calm everyone down and provide advice and exercises to help you through this. Without parents, therapy doesn't work.

From Page 17

YOUR KID'S WORLD IS RUNNING AT THE WRONG SPEED.

It can be that simple. If the world is running faster than your kid is thinking, his or her attention will fall behind. It will probably seem like that young mind is constantly wandering off. Things don't get done on time, or maybe not at all. Is he or she really behind? Maybe your kid is just on another path, or another schedule.

Or, maybe your kid is running faster than the world (that happens!). Maybe that young mind is hurtling through thoughts at a miraculous pace. They may not all be great thoughts, but they're going so fast that they'll make room for great thoughts to come along. That wonderful young mind may be so bored with a tedious classroom or the monotonous view from a moving car that it roams off into more interesting areas, exploring thoughts, places, visions. Whatever.

Sure, it's important to be in touch with the world around you, but there are many stories of people who seemed out of touch, yet somehow accomplished great things.

Maybe let some things go.

GO TO PAGE 2

41

You can put all that ADHD energy to good use playing sports.

All of these great sports figures had ADHD.
Draw a line from these athletes to their sport. (Some sports are repeated.)

Simone Biles
Pete Rose
Greg Louganis
Carl Lewis
Magic Johnson
Michael Jordan
Nolan Ryan
Muhammad Ali
Michael Phelps
Terry Bradshaw
Babe Ruth
Greg LeMond
Bruce Jenner
Tony Hawk

Skateboarding
Swimming
Gymnastics
Boxing
Baseball
Football
Cycling
Diving
Track & Field
Basketball

So go play! You don't have to become a world champion to have fun (but you might).

From Page 35

Inventors with ADHD.

Wilbur Wright and his brother Orville are thought to have had ADHD, but it didn't stop these two unlikely bicycle mechanics from inventing the first airplane.

It's not unusual for inventors to have ADHD. Inventors are, first of all, thinkers. They typically have a wide range of interests, and often these ideas come together in unusual ways and result in the creation of new things.

Here are some examples.

Alexander Graham Bell invented the telephone and had multiple other inventions.

Thomas Edison created the electric light bulb, the phonograph, and many other things.

Benjamin Franklin invented bifocals, the lightning rod, and the Franklin stove, in addition to many other accomplishments.

Louis Pasteur was involved in the creation of a number of important vaccines.

Prominent modern inventors include Woody Norris, Steve Jobs, and Dean Kamen.

Go to Page 18

WHY DON'T MY PARENTS UNDERSTAND?

It may not seem like it, but they are trying very hard.

We all have trouble dealing with other people's problems. Parents are no different in that way. You need to be patient with them sometimes.

Talk to your parents. Tell them what you're going through. Then listen to what's bothering them.

When your behaviors drive them crazy, learn what you've done and try to change that behavior.

FROM PAGE 51

HOW CAN I EXPLAIN ALL THIS TO MY TEACHER?

Your teacher already knows about ADHD and may already suspect that you have ADHD tendencies.

Ask your parents to talk to your teacher. (They may already have.)

Maybe you need more time on projects or tests. Maybe you need to walk around. Maybe a different seat will help. Or reduced homework. Sound good?

Find out if your school offers help or resources for kids with ADHD, such as an Individualized Education Plan (IEP) or a 504 Plan. Take advantage of those things.

Teachers, of course, have a lot of other students to deal with, too, so they may be busier than you think, but keep talking.

Remember, you're not looking for an excuse. You're looking for a partnership.

GO TO PAGE 46

TO READ THIS PAGE, HOLD IT UP TO A MIRROR!

MAYBE YOUR PARENTS HAVE A POINT.

If there are times when you are disruptive or overactive, that can make your mom and dad a little grumpy. Maybe you've noticed that.

It's as important for your parents to understand you as it is for you to understand them.

The big difference is that parents run the world (for now). You have to keep peace with them.

They are ALWAYS trying to understand you and your problems. You should try to understand them, too.

Sometimes they need a break, just like you do. Try to learn when to give them a little peace and quiet. They'll appreciate it.

FROM PAGE 45

WHAT WILL HAPPEN TO ME?

You will grow up. As you grow, your ADHD will become less bothersome for two reasons.

One, your brain will develop and reduce the ADHD problems.

Two, you will learn how to deal with ADHD and overcome it.

And, you will find some things that are better because of your ADHD.

When you are interested in something, you can REALLY focus on it and learn about it and get things done in that world. So, at some point the journey is to find something that really interests you.

Maybe it will start as a hobby, or a game, or even something you had to study in school. You'll learn about it and work really hard at it and you'll become really good at it. Better than most people.

You can become an expert!

GO TO PAGE 60

COOKING IS EASY. ADHD IS HARD.

If ADHD was easy, you wouldn't be reading this book. You'd already have all the answers.

But you don't. It's hard to find answers when there are so many distractions.

Nobody understands, and you're tired of being criticized. Your parents and teachers accuse you of not listening or paying attention. They say you make careless mistakes. You're disorganized, so you always lose things. You're forgetful, even about routine things in your life. You don't finish things. You've heard all this and more, over and over.

Do you fidget and squirm? Do you have trouble staying in your seat and run around when you shouldn't? Do you talk constantly when you should be quiet? Do you have trouble waiting for your turn and just blurt things out? Do you interrupt people? That's the hyperactive part.

You can beat this thing. You can show them all. You are going to succeed!

FROM PAGE 5

FOLLOW THE SPAGHETTI!

ADHD CAN MAKE YOU FEEL LIKE YOUR BRAIN IS JUST A PULSING PILE OF SPAGHETTI, WITH A CONSTANT JUMBLE OF THOUGHTS TWISTING AND TURNING IN A MAZE OF TURMOIL.

THE IMPULSIVENESS THING IS HARD. SOMETIMES YOU KNOW WHAT YOU SHOULD DO AND YOU DON'T DO IT — YOU DON'T EVEN KNOW WHY. AND SOMETIMES YOU KNOW NOT TO DO SOMETHING AND YOU DO IT ANYWAY.

BUT, YOU CAN TEACH YOURSELF TO CALM DOWN AND MAKE BETTER DECISIONS. TRAIN YOURSELF TO PAUSE BEFORE YOU ACT. START RECOGNIZING WHAT YOUR IMPULSIVENESS "FEELS LIKE," BASED ON YOUR PAST EXPERIENCE. ONCE YOU'VE LEARNED TO RECOGNIZE THE FEELING YOU CAN WORK ON CHANGING YOUR ACTIONS.

WHEN YOU DO THAT, THINGS IN YOUR LIFE WILL IMPROVE. DON'T GIVE UP. KEEP TRYING.

AND SEE IF YOU CAN FIND YOUR WAY THROUGH THE MAZE.

GO TO PAGE 58

LOTS OF ACTORS AND ENTERTAINERS HAVE CONQUERED ADHD.

Famous movie stars, comedians, and magicians harnessed their ADHD and found success. They've learned their lines and learned discipline. Steve McQueen, George C. Scott, Robin Williams, Dustin Hoffman, Harry Anderson, Henry Winkler, Danny Glover, Jim Carrey, Will Smith, Johnny Depp, Suzanne Somers, Lindsay Wagner, Silvester Stallone, Cher, Whoopi Goldberg, Tom Cruise, Mariel Hemingway, Joan Rivers, Howie Mandel, David Blaine, Tommy Smothers, Harry Belafonte, and many more.

You could be next.

FROM PAGE 19

THERE ARE MILITARY HEROES WHOSE ADHD DIDN'T SLOW THEM DOWN.

General George Patton, General Dwight D. Eisenhower, General William Westmoreland, and General Norman Schwarzkopf, plus fighter pilot heroes such as Eddie Rickenbacher & Greg Boyington.

Go to Page 44

How did you get to this page?

There is not one page in this book that sends you here.

You've been thinking out of the box. Good for you.

It's good to follow directions. It's also good to think for yourself.

Peanut Butter and Jelly Salad Recipe

1/2 head of lettuce
4 cherry tomatoes
2 scallions (chopped)
3 mushrooms (sliced)
1 carrot (sliced)
2 radishes (sliced)
2 slices of bread for croutons
2 tbsp grape jelly
3 tbsp peanut butter

Shred lettuce into bowl.
Add all the stupid veggies.
Toss it all together.
Throw it out.
Don't make the croutons.
Spread peanut butter on slice of bread.
Spread jelly on other slice of bread.
Combine bread into sandwich.
Eat sandwich.

SECRET INGREDIENTS

If you want to read this special bonus page, send an email to
SECRETPAGE@COSWORTHPUBLISHING.COM.

In return, you will receive an email that contains this special page,
and also a link to a free audiobook.

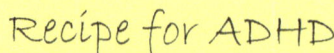

Recipe for ADHD

1 wonderful, adorable child
1 cup attention difficulty
2 tablespoons hyperactivity
1 pinch of impulsiveness

Combine ingredients.
Stir frantically until exhausted.
Salt to taste.
Simmer until grown.

ATTENTION DIFFICULTY? HYPERACTIVITY? IMPULSIVENESS?

It all sounds like quite a problem — and it is, for your parents, your teachers, your coaches, your doctors, and all the authority figures that want to control your life.

Don't worry. They're all going to lose out against the very qualities that make you ADHD.

They'll say you have attention difficulty. You don't. You simply don't pay attention to what they want you to pay attention to. You have instead turned your attention to something that interests you — if only for a short while. Then you turn your attention to something else that interests you.

The same adults who say you are hyperactive can sometimes be heard saying, "I wish I had all that energy." Being hyperactive means you can get things done — if you can concentrate.

Impulsiveness. Okay, that one can be quite a problem. You'll have to work on that.

FROM PAGE 23

54

THERE ARE THREE KINDS OF PEOPLE WITH ADHD.

1. PEOPLE WHO ARE PREDOMINANTLY INATTENTIVE

That's when your mind wanders. You have trouble organizing things or finishing things. You forget things that you should be paying attention to. You have trouble listening to people.

2. PEOPLE WHO ARE PREDOMINANTLY HYPERACTIVE

You fidget, fidget, fidget. And you talk a lot, even when you shouldn't. You move around when you should be sitting still. And you're impulsive, interrupting and talking when you should wait your turn. You're so impulsive that it causes you to have too many accidents.

3. PEOPLE WHO ARE BOTH

Lucky you. You have a combination of both types of ADHD symptoms.

So pick which one are you?

Special ADHD Style Cookies

180 pounds flour (or 600 cups)
1 quart baking soda
2 pints baking powder
12 1/2 gallons soft butter
75 pounds white sugar
17 dozen eggs
4 cups vanilla extract

Preheat oven to a million degrees (C or F).
Stir it all up super-briskly for 12 hours.
Plop onto baking pan.
Bake for 10 seconds or stop before charring.
Makes 10,000 regular cookies or 1 big one.
Caution!
Cookie(s) will be hot.

Go to Page 1

Got Anger? Frustration?

Is there sometimes a raging torrent of thoughts going through your mind?

Not surprising. With ADHD the normal frustrations that are part of growing up can be exaggerated.

It's easy to imagine that a young pianist might easily find that his or her ability to play a piece is beyond the reach of his or her tiny fingers.

It's easy to imagine that a young artist might have a visual sense that far outstrips his or her ability to express a perfect image onto paper or canvas.

A young carpenter might find that a hammer more easily hits a finger than a nail.

Frustration can lead to bad behavior, and that creates a challenge for everyone — not just parents and teachers, but friends.

So, it's understandable that a young student with ADHD can easily fall behind and feel like it's all over — there's no way to catch up.

Even simple things can seem worse for any kid with ADHD.

Super-quick Pheasant Under Glass Recipe (Fasison Sous Cloche)

1 pheasant, defeathered & deboned (or substitute 4 frozen burgers)	Flatten pheasant with a mallet. That's enough...
8 shallots (fresh or canned)	Stop with the mallet!
1/2 cup fresh lemon juice	(You can smash something else later.)
1 can mushrooms (opened)	Might as well smash the mushrooms and truffles.
2 truffles (not the chocolate kind)	Rub the breasts with everything else.
3 tbsp *unsalted* butter	Except maybe the butter. Melt it. Probably in a skillet.
1 pinch of salt (for the butter)	
1/4 dash cayenne pepper	Cook the pheasant (or burgers) in the butter and cream.
1/2 cup chicken broth (or substitute pheasant broth)	Saute shallots and mushrooms. Add them, too.
1/2 cup cream (not ice cream)	Cover with a glass dome. Or eat the burgers.

From Page 37

56

Doubts?

It's not much help to hear that things will get better when you're an adult. You want things to get better now. That's perfectly reasonable.

It's going to be hard.

But you can do it. Start by getting through today.

ADHD struggles can lead to self-esteem issues that can only be fixed by you.

It helps to have positive thoughts. Think about a teacher or friend who has helped you and smile. Is there someone who encourages you more than others do? Listen to them. Is there a school subject that you like? Focus on enjoying it. Is there someone who tries to help you or understand your troubles? Thank them. You get the idea. Try it.

Go to Page 8

Tools for ADHD.

People with ADHD get things done — once they've learned to focus. Your parents may not like these ideas at first. Ask them to let you try them and see if they help.

You may find that, in general, your stimulation level may need to be high in order for you to concentrate. It sounds weird, but since kids with ADHD often have low dopamine levels, a little caffeine can help a kid's concentration by raising the dopamine level. Too much, obviously, can cause trouble though. Be careful and wise.

Doodling or drawing in classroom situations can be helpful in enabling you to listen, learn, and think. And they're harmless. Folding or ripping paper may help you retain information. Your teacher won't like it, but when you're at home you can try bouncing your legs or drumming on your desk. There are computer apps that will read text from a book aloud. Or, try "Study with me" on YouTube.

If you lose things a lot, learn to always use a book bag, or a backpack, or anything that will give you room to keep everything you need there. Pencils, paper, keys, tissues, cell phone, medicines, snacks, whatever. Make a habit of ALWAYS putting things there. Then remember to take it with you so you'll have everything you need.

Does it feel like your mind rages at low levels of ambient sound? Silence can be even worse. So, you may need the sound level to be high to study or learn. That may mean MUSIC will help. Maybe LOUD music! (with headphones...)

Go for a run before school. Take lots of breaks. Drink water. Find tools that work for you!

From Page 49

Try the Pomodoro Study Method.

It's simple, but you have to stick with it.

Organize your work into small, doable blocks called tomatoes. Yep. Tomatoes.

Set a timer. (It doesn't have to be a tomato timer.)

Study for 25 minutes with no interruptions for talking, texting, social media, YouTube, etc.

Take a break for 5 minutes.

Study for 25 minutes with no interruptions for talking, texting, social media, YouTube, etc.

Take a break for 5 minutes.

Study for 25 minutes with no interruptions for talking, texting, social media, YouTube, etc.

Take a break for 10 or 15 minutes. Repeat as needed.

If your work takes more time than that, break it down into smaller pieces.

If you don't have that much work at one time, combine it with other small tasks into one big beautiful tomato.

Go to Page 24

Money Management

Spending money is fun. Right?

That makes it particularly tough for anyone with ADHD and impulse control issues to be sensible (that means boring) about money.

Kids don't usually have a lot of money, and when they get some it's hard to hang on to it, so this is the time to learn good money management practices and put them to work.

That means you're going to have to think about money—before you spend it.

Get organized. Start building good money habits with planning, focus, and follow-through.

A little planning will help. Keep track of what money you have and where it's going.

Pay attention (easier said than done) because if you have impulse control issues, you're definitely going to have money management issues.

Don't get excited about your purchases and forget about paying attention to where your money is going.

From Page 47

Sadly, money management only gets easy when you run completely out of money, but you definitely don't want to do that.

It will be easier to keep up with your money if you open a checking account, particularly if it comes with a debit card for your purchases.

And, a savings account will help you save for bigger purchases, or just save up some money for the future.

Dealing with money is a lot like dealing with numbers in general, but when money equals zero, it's gone forever.

Be careful. Be prudent. Be boring.

GO TO PAGE 62

Dessert!

No cookbook is complete without dessert to top things off.

Here's the happy ending. You're going to get better.

As you grow up, your ADHD tendencies will reduce. They may not go away entirely, but you'll learn to recognize them and to control them.

Things will slow down enough that you can think about them and make good decisions.

You'll learn how to focus your attention enough to get things done, but not so much that other things are neglected.

It may not happen as quickly as you (and your parents) wish, but thankfully it happens.

Just like all the ADHD success stories down through history, you will learn to turn liabilities into capabilities. You will use your special qualities to help in your life.

Enjoy.

From Page 61

You've seen lots of lists of successful people with ADHD.

Which of those lists would you like to be on?

You don't have to be a famous writer or actor, an accomplished artist or musician, a brilliant physicist or scientist, a world champion athlete or even a great chef.

There are other lists that didn't make this book: great moms and dads, great teachers, coaches, doctors, and many others.

ADHD is a problem, but there is a solution — YOU!

You can solve it with determination and hard work.

Get some help where you can, share your story, and persevere.

Some day, you'll be on the list of your choosing.

Congratulations.

THE END

Go Out and Play!

About the Author

His plan was to write a regular book about ADHD, but then he got hungry.

So, it turned into a cookbook, but by then he'd already eaten.

Before he could finish, the printer stopped working. Probably out of paper or ink.

He started to fix it, but "SpongeBob" was on the TV, so that took a while.

Then the dog needed help romping out in the yard.

Naturally, there was a trip to the bathroom, too. It went pretty quick.

He had to bring in the day's mail and go through it all. Mostly bills.

That reminded him to check his email. Just junk, as usual. And no new book reviews either.

That was when the phone rang, which was a spam call, but took way too long and he got really mad and thought maybe he should write them a letter, but that was too much work and by then he was hungry again, so the cookbook idea resurfaced and here it is (if it's really finished).

More later?

THE **DYSLEXIC HANBDOOK**

Genius Edition!

LARGE PRINT - BIG PICTURES

The **I Hate to Read** Book

Jimmy Huston

THE **OCD** FUNBOOK

REALLY?

Rat BLEEP and Alien Poop

NOT FOR PARENTS AT ALL

A Non-Illustrated Picture Book

WARNING! The actual photographs of all Aliens have been CENSORED, so you will have to draw your own pictures.

Non-Cookbooks from Cosworth Publishing

www.cosworthpublishing.com

...and **I Hate Math 2** Who Needs It?

Jimmy Huston

The Snake Test

☐ True? ☐ False? ☐ Maybe

THE BIG BEAUTIFUL BOOK OF **BURPING BELCHING & BARFING**

CUSSING for KIDS!

Etiquette for the Profane

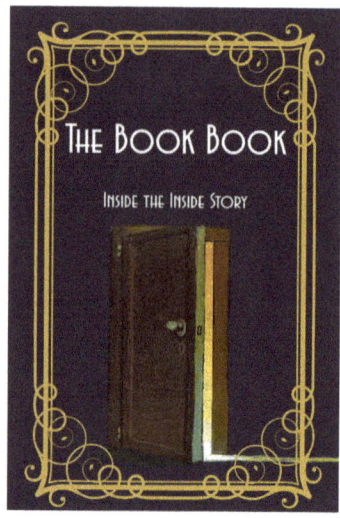

THE BOOK BOOK

INSIDE THE INSIDE STORY

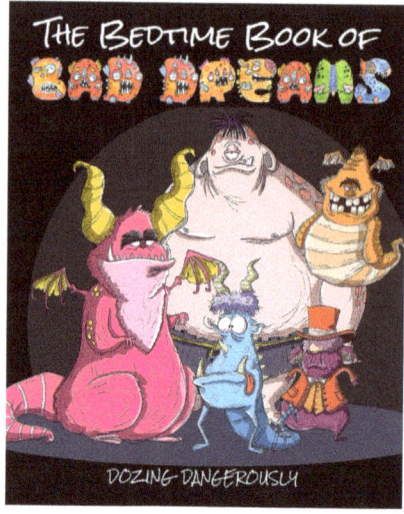

THE BEDTIME BOOK OF BAD DREAMS

DOZING DANGEROUSLY

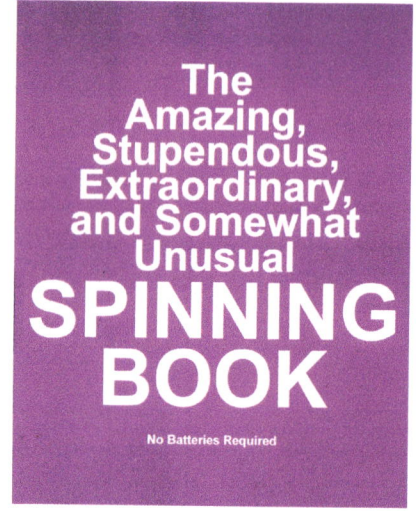

The Amazing, Stupendous, Extraordinary, and Somewhat Unusual SPINNING BOOK

No Batteries Required

Wisdom of the Aged

PG-65

Dead Is the New Sick

An Insider's Guide to Senility, Paranoia & Curmudgery

Jimmy Huston

Non-Cookbooks from Cosworth Publishing

www.cosworthpublishing.com

DON'T GO TO COLLEGE, GO TO EUROPE FOR LESS

Jimmy Huston

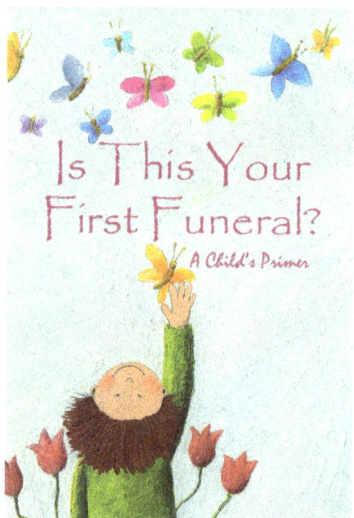

Is This Your First Funeral?

A Child's Primer

Nate-Nate the Christmas Snake

Baby's First Instruction Manual

PG-½

How To Be the Center of the Universe

Find it wherever good books are dreaded.

The I Hate to Read Book
Jimmy Huston

If you're reading this, you will not like this book. It's not for you.

This book is for all the people who are *not* reading this.

They won't like it either, but it's short.

They'll like that.

*"I didn't actually read this book. If I had, I would have loved it —
but I never will."*
Billy

*"'Hate' isn't a strong enough word for me. I loathe reading. I
don't even like looking at pictures — which there are none of."*
Wally

"This isn't what I wrote about this stupid book."
Zane

*"This is an excellent coffee table book, if your coffee table hates
to read."*
Solomon

"This book made my teacher cry."
David

"My son loved this book. He said it was delicious."
Mr. Jones

"THIS BOOK IS SO DUMB THAT I COULD'VE WRITTEN IT."
Jimmy

www.i-hate-to-read.com

How to Write This Book!
You're going to be the author.

_____
(Write your name here.)

The Attention Deficit Disorder Hyperactive Cookbook
PUZZLE EDITION

Why Can't Mommy Spend More Time with Me?

SO YOU REALLY WANT A DOG?
A Kid's Guide to Getting a Dog

Learn What You Need to Know to Show Your Parents You're Ready

Lynn Mills

More Books from Cosworth Publishing

www.cosworthpublishing.com

Engelmann the Footloose Christmas Spruce

Lynn Mills

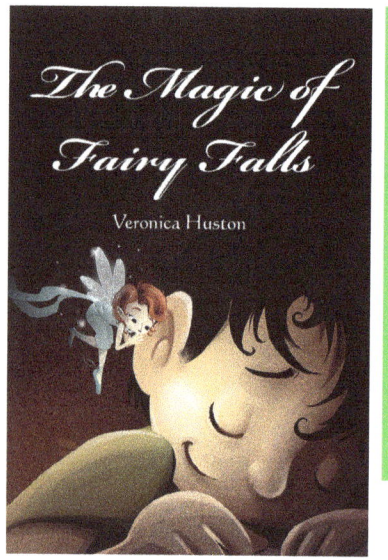

The Magic of Fairy Falls

Veronica Huston

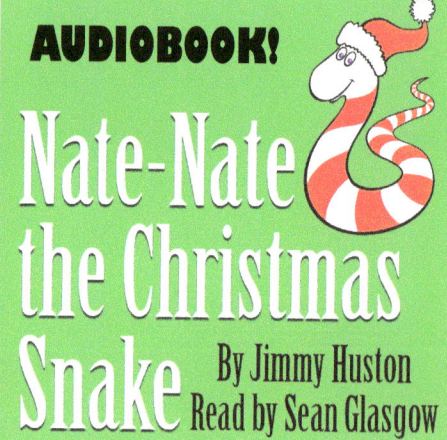

AUDIOBOOK!
Nate-Nate the Christmas Snake
By Jimmy Huston
Read by Sean Glasgow

That Damn Little Angel!

Dead Is the New Sick
An Insider's Guide to Senility, Paranoia, & Curmudgery

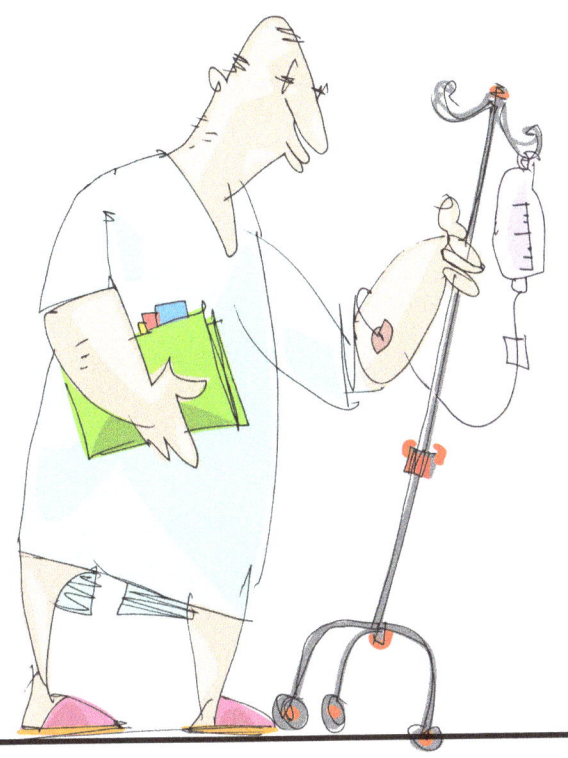

"Warmly affectionate elder abuse."
— Methuselah

"Sadly funny..."
— Sophocles

"The Pet Rock of western literature."
— Anon.

"I don't feel so good."
— John Doe

Top 10 Warnings

1. Hospice is a crock. Keep a jug of water under the bed.
2. Write a will.
4. Hide it.
5. Don't walk toward the light.
6. Did you take your meds today?
7. Are you sure?
8. What happened to Number 3?
9. Eat a pie.
10. If there has ever been something you wanted to do, but didn't for whatever reason, now is the time to do it! Start with this book!

www.deadsick.com

Books for Grownups from Cosworth Publishing

www.cosworthpublishing.com

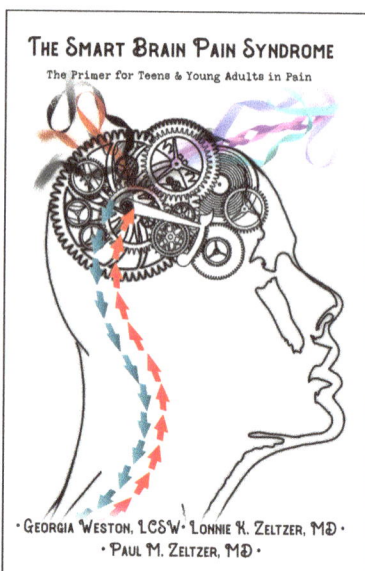

A groundbreaking new book. Three experts explain chronic pain to teens and parents, including using creative outlets to displace the pain.

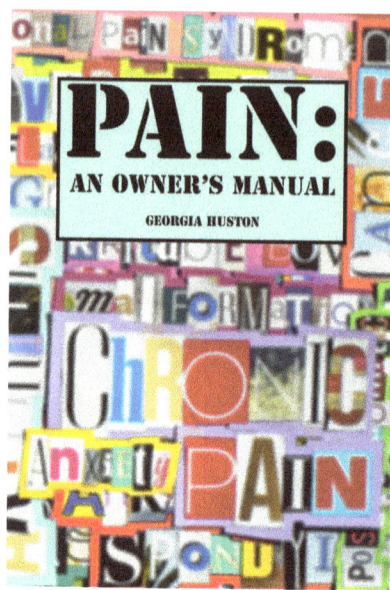

A young pain victim's inspirational and informative conversations with a variety of pain sufferers and specialists. Doctors should read this at their own risk.

At 14, Georgia developed mysterious chronic pain. This book chronicles that dark time and follows her inspirational journey back to health and happiness.

A practical guide for the person who is confronted by the possible suicide of a friend or family member.

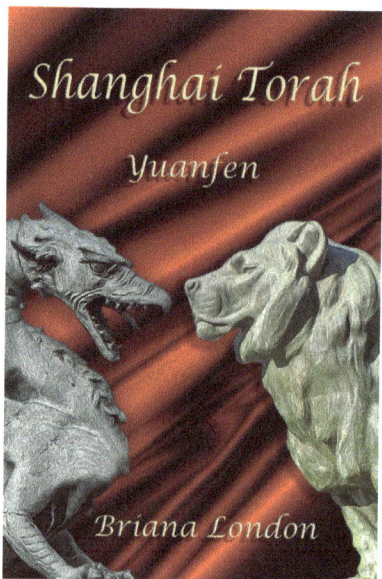

A young Jewish scribe flees WWII Europe with his in-progress Torah, escaping into China under Japanese occupation.

AUDIOBOOK

A powerful reading of Georgia's harrowing experiences as a young teen suffering chronic pain. Hearing it all out loud brings new power and meaning to this true-life story.

Thanks for buying, borrowing, or swiping this wonderful book.

At Cosworth Publishing we truly appreciate that, and in return, we'd like to offer you one of our E-books absolutely free—and worth every penny.

Just let us know that you want it, and we'll make sure that you get it. Let us know which book you read so we don't send you the same one.

Send an email to *office@cosworthpublishing.com*.

Then, from time to time, we will let you know via email when we have a new book that you might be interested in.

We won't do that very often because we're basically pretty lazy, and we don't produce very many new books.

Reviews are usually appreciated.

www.ingramcontent.com/pod-product-compliance
Lightning Source LLC
Chambersburg PA
CBHW041519120626
46551CB00018B/2494